What's in this book

This book belongs to

_____

颜色真好玩 Colour fun

学习内容 Contents

沟通 Communication

说说颜色
Talk about colours

生词 New words

★	红色	red
★	黄色	yellow
★	蓝色	blue
★	绿色	green
★	黑色	black
★	白色	white
★	灰色	grey
★	吗	(question word)
	颜色	colour

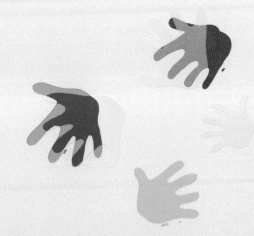

句式 Sentence patterns

这是黄色吗?
Is this yellow?

你喜欢绿色吗?
Do you like green?

跨学科学习 Project

认识动物保护色及
具有变色能力的动物
Learn about camouflage and
colour-changing animals

文化 Cultures

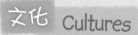

红色在中国文化中的意义
The colour red in Chinese culture

Get ready

1 How many colours are there on the palette?

2 What happens when different colours are mixed?

3 What is your favourite colour?

huáng sè

黄色

这是黄色吗？

黄色加蓝色，颜色会变吗？

黄色加蓝色，会变成绿色。

hēi sè
黑色

bái sè
白色

黑色加白色，变成什么颜色？

灰色
huī sè

黑色加白色，变成灰色。

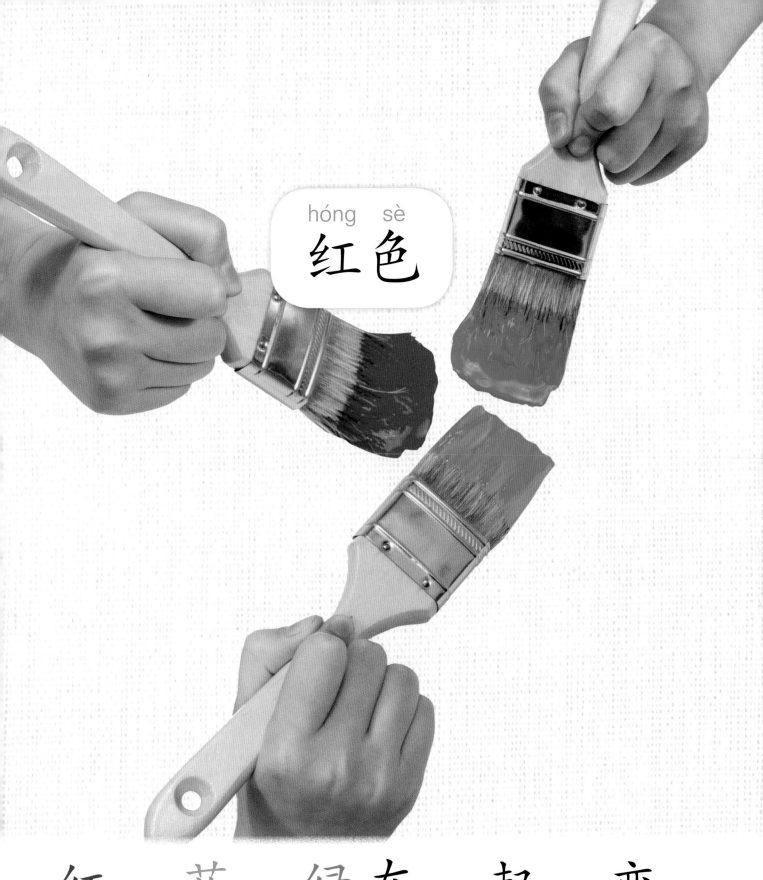

红色

红、蓝、绿在一起，变成什么颜色？

Let's think

1 Look at the colour mixing picture and think. Put a tick or a cross.

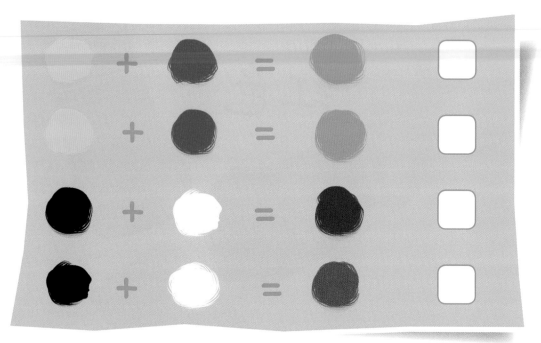

2 What colour do you get when mixing red, blue and green together? Try it out on the dinosaur.

New words

1 Learn the new words.

灰色 吗 黑色 白色 黄色 红色 绿色 蓝色 颜色

2 Match the words to the pictures. Write the letters.

a 红色 b 绿色 c 蓝色 d 黑色 e 黄色 f 白色 g 灰色

听听说说 Listen and say

 1 Listen carefully. Put a tick or a cross.

 2 Look at the pictures. Listen to the sto...

① 这是什么颜色？

黑色。

③ 你喜欢什么颜色？

我喜欢黄色。

...nd say.

3 Match and say. Colour the pictures.

你喜欢什么颜色?

是的,这是白色的鸟。

这是白色的鸟吗?

我喜欢黄色。

不,我喜欢红色的苹果。

你喜欢绿色的苹果吗?

Task

Tick the colours of the flags and say.

它有红色和黄色。

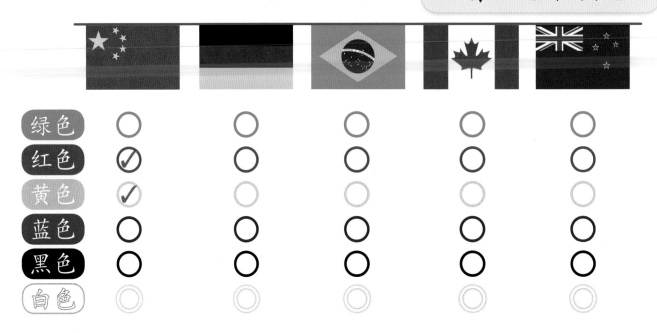

绿色	○	○	○	○	○
红色	✓	○	○	○	○
黄色	✓	○	○	○	○
蓝色	○	○	○	○	○
黑色	○	○	○	○	○
白色	○	○	○	○	○

Game

Work with your friend. Listen and point to the correct objects.

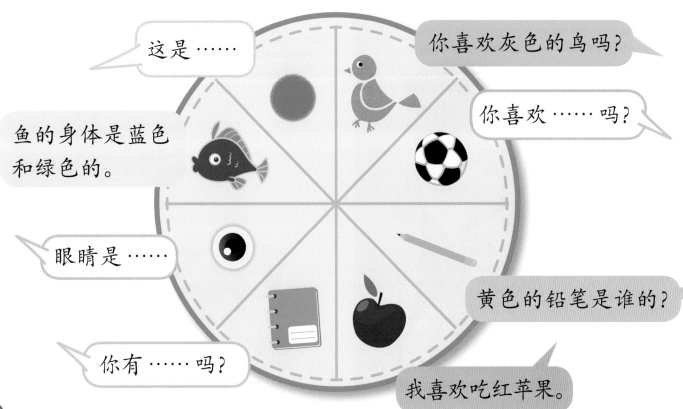

这是……

你喜欢灰色的鸟吗？

鱼的身体是蓝色和绿色的。

你喜欢……吗？

眼睛是……

黄色的铅笔是谁的？

你有……吗？

我喜欢吃红苹果。

Song

🎧 05 Listen and sing.

红黄蓝绿黑白灰，

红加黄，变成橙。

黄加蓝，变成绿。

黑加白，变成灰。

红黄蓝绿黑白灰，

变变颜色真好玩。

课堂用语 Classroom language

现在开始。
Start now.

涂颜色。
Colour the picture.

写一写 Write

1 Learn and trace the stroke.

撇折

2 Learn the component. Circle 纟 in the characters.

纟 红 绿 结 纸

3 Circle the characters with 纟.

红 纸 结 线 绿 孩 黄 蓝 颜 鱼

4 Trace and write the character.

5 Write and say.

我喜欢  色。

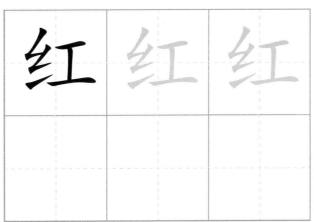

汉字小常识 Did you know?

Study the characters. Colour the meaning component red and the sound component green.

Many characters are made up of two components. One gives a clue to the meaning, while the other to the sound.

 妈 星 睛 绿

Cultures

1 When you think of the colour red, what comes to your mind?
Tick the boxes.

2 Do you know the meaning of red in Chinese culture?

Chinese Palaces

Chinese New Year

Wedding

Red is a popular colour in China. It means glory, happiness and good luck. You see it a lot during Chinese celebrations and festivals.

1 Some animals can change colour to protect themselves. Read and write the letters.

Octopuses change colour to communicate with their friends or when frightened.

A   B   C   D   E   F

☐ 我变成灰色。

☐ 我变成蓝色。

Chameleons change the colour of their skin to match the surroundings.

☐ 冬天来了，我变成白色。

Arctic foxes change the colour of their fur with the seasons.

☐ 我变成黑色。

☐ 我变成绿色。

2 Paint your hands and play with your friends.

我的翅膀是蓝色的吗？

我有灰色的长鼻子。

温习 Checkpoint

1 Look at the wheel and answer the questions.

⭐**8** 香蕉是什么颜色？

⭐**7** 我有红色的身体吗？

⭐**6** Write 'red' in Chinese.

⭐**5** 我的身体是什么颜色？

色加什么颜色，
成绿色？

⭐2 我是蓝色
的吗？

⭐3 你喜欢什
么颜色？

⭐4 你喜欢我吗？

2 Work with your friend. Colour the stars and the chillies.

Words and sentences	说	读	写
红（色）	☆	☆	☆
黄色	☆	☆	🌶
蓝色	☆	☆	🌶
绿色	☆	☆	🌶
黑色	☆	☆	🌶
白色	☆	☆	🌶
灰色	☆	☆	🌶
吗	☆	☆	🌶
颜色	☆	🌶	🌶
这是红色吗？	☆	☆	🌶
你喜欢绿色吗？	☆	☆	🌶

Talk about the colours	☆

3 What does your teacher say?

21

分享 Sharing

Words I remember

红色	hóng sè	red
黄色	huáng sè	yellow
蓝色	lán sè	blue
绿色	lǜ sè	green
黑色	hēi sè	black
白色	bái sè	white
灰色	huī sè	grey
吗	ma	(question word)
颜色	yán sè	colour

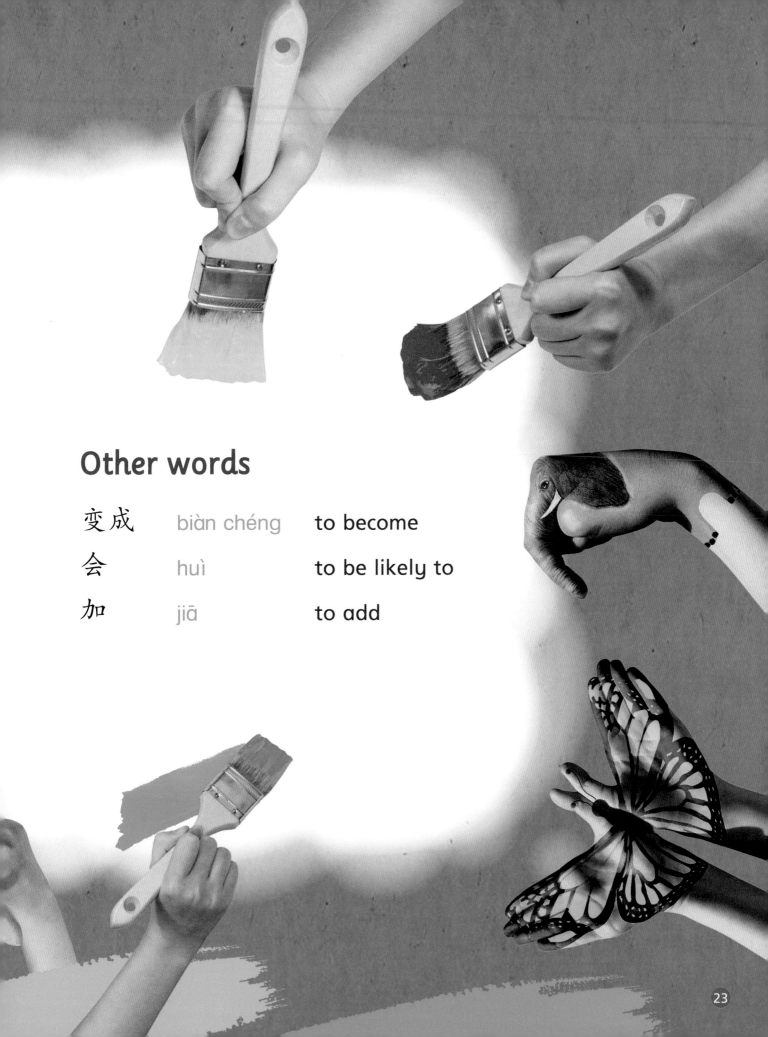

Other words

变成	biàn chéng	to become
会	huì	to be likely to
加	jiā	to add

Oxford University Press is a department of the University of Oxford.
It furthers the University's objective of excellence in research, scholarship,
and education by publishing worldwide. Oxford is a registered trade mark of
Oxford University Press in the UK and in certain other countries

Published in Hong Kong by
Oxford University Press (China) Limited
39th Floor, One Kowloon, 1 Wang Yuen Street, Kowloon Bay,
Hong Kong

Illustrated by Anne Lee and Wildman

Photographs for reproduction permitted by Dreamstime.com

China National Publications Import & Export (Group) Corporation is an authorized distributor of
Oxford Elementary Chinese.

Please contact content@cnpiec.com.cn or 86-10-65856782

ISBN: 978-0-19-082146-3

10 9 8 7 6 5 4 3 2